THE
ROSARY

THE GREAT WEAPON OF THE 21ST CENTURY

THIS BOOK BELONGS TO:

_____

THE ROSARY

THE GREAT WEAPON OF THE 21ST CENTURY

A Guide to Praying the Rosary

America Needs Fatima
P.O. Box 341
Hanover, PA 17331

Book Design: Jennifer Bohdal
Cover Design: Elizabeth Ferraz
Rosary Mystery Paintings: Jose Roberto Dias Tavares

ISBN: 978-1-877905-19-3
Library of Congress Control Number: 2019954700

B96

Printed in the United States of America

"Pray the Rosary every day in order to obtain peace for the world."

— OUR LADY OF FATIMA, MAY 13, 1917

INTRODUCTION

The title of our book, *The Rosary, the Great Weapon of the 21st Century* was chosen for a specific reason. Throughout history, it is noticeable that whenever a people or a nation is at risk of an imminent calamity as a consequence of moral regression, Divine Providence will many times propose a supernatural solution.

In the Old Testament, when the people of Israel were being bitten by poisoned snakes sent by God to chastise them for their infidelities, Moses prayed for his people. In response, God told Moses to make a bronze snake on a pole. Anyone who wanted to be saved from the snake bites had only to look upon the bronze snake on the pole held by Moses and their health would be restored. To this day, the symbol is used for healing institutions and frequently seen in hospitals.

In the seventeenth century, the Sacred Heart of Jesus appeared to Saint Margaret Mary Alacoque, asking the French king through her to have France consecrated to His Sacred Heart. The king did not do it and exactly 100 years later, the French Revolution broke out, causing the most sorrowful period in French history, with thousands of killings and a severe persecution against the Church. When King Louis XVI was imprisoned by the French revolutionaries, he did what his predecessor had neglected and consecrated France to the Sacred Heart of Jesus from his prison; but it was too late. The French know this story well, for they built the enormous basilica of Montmartre. Visitors to the basilica can read an engraving on a huge bronze plaque which states that the basilica was built and dedicated to the Sacred Heart of Jesus in reparation for the sins of the French Revolution.

Much like seventeenth century France, our modern world moves towards its own demise by the abandonment of morals, destruction of the family and turning its back on God in every way imaginable. But again, as so many times before in history, God has sent a messenger to give us the remedy. In 1917, He sent His own Mother to Fatima. She came to warn us of what will come if we do not change course; and as the solution she asked us to "Pray the Rosary."

The Rosary is therefore the Great Weapon of the twenty-first century. The Rosary has already proven itself in history as a most powerful weapon for good and its power is indeed infinite. It is joined to the most powerful and pure hands of the Blessed Virgin Mary in heaven, to whose desires the Holy Trinity is most attentive.

As individuals, besides fighting bravely in the Cultural Wars, we must pray the Rosary faithfully to fulfill what Our Lady of Fatima asked us to do when she appeared in Fatima to the three shepherd children. Pray the Rosary, pray it well, get others to do the same and watch as your life and the world are transformed!

Robert E. Ritchie
Executive Director,
America Needs Fatima

Prayers
of the # Holy Rosary
and # More

How to PRAY the ROSARY

1. Make the *Sign of the Cross* and say the *Apostles Creed*.

2. Say the *Our Father*.

3. Say three *Hail Marys*.

4. Say the *Glory Be*. Announce the first Mystery and say the *Our Father*.

5. Say ten *Hail Marys* while meditating on the Mystery.

6. Say the *Glory Be*. Say the Fatima prayers. Announce the second Mystery and say the *Our Father*.

7. Say ten *Hail Marys* while meditating on the Mystery.

8. Say the *Glory Be*. Say the Fatima prayers. Announce the third Mystery and say the *Our Father*.

9. Say ten *Hail Marys* while meditating on the Mystery.

10. Say the *Glory Be*. Say the Fatima prayers. Announce the fourth Mystery and say the *Our Father*.

11. Say ten *Hail Marys* while meditating on the Mystery.

12. Say the *Glory Be*. Say the Fatima prayers. Announce the fifth Mystery and say the *Our Father*.

13. Say ten *Hail Marys* while meditating on the Mystery.

14. Say the *Glory Be*. Say the Fatima prayers. Say the *Hail Holy Queen* and the prayer to St. Michael the Archangel.

"Pray the rosary every day to obtain peace for the world and the end of the war," Our Lady said to the three young shepherds of Fatima on May 13, 1917. In each of the six apparitions, she insisted on the necessity of the daily rosary.

The rosary begins with the Sign of the Cross and the Apostles' Creed, followed by an Our Father, three Hail Marys and a Glory Be.

At this point the intentions are given, and then five mysteries are prayed.

Each mystery is announced and then an Our Father, ten Hail Marys and a Glory Be are prayed, while meditating on the mystery. This is followed by the prayer requested by Our Lady of Fatima: "O My Jesus..."

When praying the rosary it is important to remember to meditate on the life of Our Lord. Each decade or mystery corresponds to an episode in the life of Our Lord Jesus Christ or of the Blessed Virgin Mary.

When praying the Hail Mary it is important to pronounce the Holy Name of Jesus with great reverence. This means that when the rosary is being prayed in a group, before joining in with the second part of the Hail Mary, those answering the prayers should wait until after whoever is leading has finished the first part. Otherwise the Holy Name of Jesus will not be uttered and meditated upon with due reverence.

At Fatima, Our Lady requested that we pray one rosary of five decades every day. It is good and praiseworthy to pray more than one rosary each day if and when possible.

PRAYERS *of the* ROSARY

The Sign of the Cross

In the name of the Father, and of the Son, and of the Holy Ghost. Amen.

The Apostles' Creed

I believe in God, the Father Almighty, Creator of Heaven and earth, and in Jesus Christ, His only Son, Our Lord, Who was conceived by the Holy Ghost, born of the Virgin Mary, suffered under Pontius Pilate, was crucified, died, and was buried. He descended into Hell; the third day He rose again from the dead; He ascended into Heaven, and sitteth at the right hand of God, the Father Almighty; from thence He shall come to judge the living and the dead. I believe in the Holy Ghost, the Holy Catholic Church, the communion of saints, the forgiveness of sins, the resurrection of the body, and life everlasting. Amen.

The Our Father

Our Father, Who art in Heaven, hallowed be Thy name; Thy kingdom come, Thy will be done on earth as it is in Heaven. Give us this day our daily bread, and forgive us our trespasses, as we forgive those who trespass against us, and lead us not into temptation, but deliver us from evil. Amen.

The Hail Mary

Hail, Mary, full of grace, the Lord is with thee. Blessed art thou among women, and blessed is the fruit of thy womb, Jesus. Holy Mary, Mother of God, pray for us sinners, now and at the hour of our death. Amen.

The Glory Be

Glory be to the Father, and to the Son, and to the Holy Ghost, as it was in the beginning, is now, and ever shall be, world without end. Amen.

The O My Jesus (The Fatima Prayer)

O my Jesus, forgive us our sins, save us from the fire of Hell, lead all souls to Heaven, especially those in most need of Thy mercy.

The Hail Holy Queen

Hail Holy Queen, Mother of Mercy, our life, our sweetness and our hope! To thee do we cry, poor banished children of Eve. To thee do we send up our sighs, mourning and weeping in this valley of tears. Turn then, most gracious advocate, thine eyes of mercy towards us, and after this our exile, show unto us the blessed fruit of thy womb, Jesus. O clement, O loving, O sweet Virgin Mary.

V. Pray for us, O holy Mother of God.

R. That we may be made worthy of the promises of Christ.

Let us pray. O God, Whose only-begotten Son, by His life, death, and resurrection, has purchased for us the rewards of eternal life; grant, we beseech Thee, that meditating upon these mysteries of the most holy rosary of the Blessed Virgin Mary, we may imitate what they contain and obtain what they promise. Through the same Christ Our Lord. Amen.

Sub Tuum Praesidium

We fly to thy patronage, O holy Mother of God; despise not our petitons in our necessities, but deliver us from all dangers, O glorious and Blessed Virgin.

The Litany of the Blessed Virgin Mary

Lord, have mercy on us.
Christ, have mercy on us.
Lord, have mercy on us. Christ, hear us.
Christ, graciously hear us.

God the Father of heaven, *have mercy on us.*
God the Son, Redeemer of the world, *have mercy on us.*
God the Holy Ghost, *have mercy on us.*
Holy Trinity, one God, *have mercy on us.*
Holy Mary, *pray for us.* (repeat *'pray for us'* after each invocation.)
Holy Mother of God,
Holy Virgin of virgins,
Mother of Christ,
Mother of divine grace,
Mother most pure,
Mother most chaste,
Mother inviolate,
Mother undefiled,
Mother most amiable,
Mother most admirable,
Mother of good counsel,
Mother of our Creator,
Mother of our Savior,
Virgin most prudent,
Virgin most venerable,
Virgin most renowned,
Virgin most powerful,
Virgin most merciful,
Virgin most faithful,
Mirror of justice,
Seat of wisdom,
Cause of our joy,
Spiritual vessel,
Vessel of honor,
Singular vessel of devotion,
Mystical rose,
Tower of David,
Tower of ivory,
House of gold,

Ark of the covenant,
Gate of heaven,
Morning star,
Health of the sick,
Refuge of sinners,
Comforter of the afflicted,
Help of Christians,
Queen of angels,
Queen of patriarchs,
Queen of prophets,
Queen of apostles,
Queen of martyrs,
Queen of confessors,
Queen of virgins,
Queen of all saints,
Queen conceived without original sin,
Queen assumed into heaven,
Queen of the most Holy Rosary,
Queen of families,
Queen of peace,

V. Lamb of God, Who takest away the sins of the world,
R. *Spare us, O Lord.*
V. Lamb of God, Who takest away the sins of the world,
R. *Graciously hear us, O Lord.*
V. Lamb of God, Who takest away the sins of the world,
R. *Have mercy on us.*
V. Pray for us, O Holy Mother of God.
R. *That we may be made worthy of the promises of Christ.*

Let us pray. Grant unto us, Thy servants, we beseech Thee, O Lord God, at all times to enjoy health of soul and body; and by the glorious intercession of Blessed Mary, ever virgin, when freed from the sorrows of this present life, to enter into that joy which hath no end. Through Christ Our Lord. Amen.

The Memorare

Remember, O most gracious Virgin Mary, that never was it known that anyone who fled to thy protection, implored thy help, or sought thy intercession, was left unaided. Inspired by this confidence, I fly unto thee, O Virgin of virgins, my Mother! To thee do I come, before thee I stand, sinful and sorrowful. O Mother of the Word Incarnate, despise not my petitions, but in thy mercy, hear and answer me. Amen.

The Magnificat

My soul doth magnify the Lord, and my spirit hath rejoiced in God my Savior.

Because He hath regarded the humility of His handmaid.

For behold, from henceforth all generations shall call me blessed.

Because He that is mighty hath done great things to me, and holy is His Name.

And His Mercy is from generation unto generations, to them that fear Him.

He hath shewed might in His arm.

He hath scattered the proud in the conceit of their heart.

He hath put down the mighty from their seat, and hath exalted the humble.

He hath filled the hungry with good things, and the rich He hath sent empty away.

He hath received Israel His servant, being mindful of His mercy.

As He spoke to our fathers, to Abraham and to his seed for ever.

Glory be to the Father, and to the Son, and to the Holy Ghost, as it was in the beginning, is now, and ever shall be, world without end. Amen.

MEExDITATIONS *for the* BEGINNING *of the* ROSARY

Saint Louis de Montfort's Summary of the Life,
Death and Glory of Jesus and Mary in the Holy Rosary

Creed:
1. Faith in the presence of God.
2. Faith in the Gospel.
3. Faith in and obedience to the Pope as the Vicar of Jesus Christ.

Our Father:
The unity of the one, true and living God.

First Hail Mary:
In honor of the Eternal Father, Who begets the Son in contemplating Himself.

Second Hail Mary:
In honor of the Eternal Word, Who is equal to the Father, with Whom He produces the Holy Ghost.

Third Hail Mary:
In honor of the Holy Ghost, Who proceeds from the Father and the Son by way of love.

MEDITATIONS
on the MYSTERIES *of the*
HOLY ROSARY

BY ST. LOUIS MARIE GRIGNION DE MONTFORT

Statue of Saint Louis de Montfort
at Saint Peter's Basilica, Rome

FIRST JOYFUL MYSTERY
The ANNUNCIATION

In this mystery we contemplate the Virgin Mary being greeted by the angel, who announces that she is to conceive and give birth to Christ, our Redeemer.

Let us ask the Virgin of virgins, by the holy joy that filled her Immaculate Heart, to drive from our souls the discouragement and harmful sadness caused by the difficulties of daily life in this our neopagan world.

Our Father: God's immense charity.

10 Hail Marys:
1. The unfortunate state of disobedient Adam, his just condemnation, and that of all his children.
2. The desires of the Patriarchs and Prophets who asked for the Messias.
3. The wishes and prayers of the Most Holy Virgin, which hastened the coming of the Messias, and her marriage to Saint Joseph.
4. The charity of the Eternal Father, Who gave us His Son.
5. The love of the Son, Who gave Himself for us.
6. The Archangel Gabriel's mission and salutation.
7. Mary's virginal fear.
8. The Most Holy Virgin's faith and consent.
9. The creation of the soul and the formation of the body of Jesus Christ in the womb of Mary by the Holy Ghost.
10. The angels' adoration of the Incarnate Word in the womb of Mary.

Second Joyful Mystery
The VISITATION

In this mystery we contemplate the Mother of the Creator going to visit her cousin Saint Elizabeth, whose son, Saint John the Baptist, trembled with joy in the womb upon hearing the voice of Mary.

Let us ask the Mother of Good Counsel that we too may tremble with joy and devotion when the call of grace makes itself heard in the interior of our souls.

Our Father: God's adorable majesty.

10 Hail Marys:
1. The joy of the Heart of Mary, and the dwelling of the Incarnate Word in her womb for nine months.
2. The sacrifice Jesus Christ made of Himself to the Father on entering this world.
3. The delights of Jesus in the humble and virginal womb of Mary, and those of Mary in the possession of her God.
4. Saint Joseph's doubt concerning Mary's maternity.
5. The election of the chosen ones, decided between Jesus and Mary in her womb.
6. The fervor of Mary in her visit to Saint Elizabeth.
7. The salutation of Mary and the sanctification of Saint John the Baptist and his mother, Saint Elizabeth.
8. The Most Holy Virgin's gratitude toward God in the Magnificat.
9. Her charity and humility in serving her cousin.
10. The mutual dependence of Jesus and Mary and the dependence we should have on each of them.

THIRD JOYFUL MYSTERY
The NATIVITY

In this mystery we contemplate Our God, born of the Virgin Mary in Bethlehem, and laid in a manger because there was no room in the inn.

Let us ask Jesus, Mary and Joseph to give us the piety, serenity and fortitude that emanate from the holy grotto of Bethlehem.

Our Father: God's inexhaustible riches.

10 Hail Marys:
1. The scorn and rejection Mary and Joseph endured in Bethlehem.
2. The poverty of the stable wherein God came to the world.
3. Mary's high contemplation and surpassing love at the moment of Our Lord's Birth.
4. The Eternal Word's departure from the womb of Mary while maintaining her virginity.
5. The angels' adoration and hymnody at the birth of Jesus Christ.
6. The captivating beauty of His divine infancy.
7. The coming of the shepherds to the stable with their small presents.
8. The circumcision of Jesus Christ, and His affectionate pains.
9. The imposition of the Name of Jesus, and its grandeur.
10. The adoration of the Magi Kings, and their gifts.

FOURTH JOYFUL MYSTERY
The PRESENTATION

In this mystery we contemplate the Virgin Mary carrying her Son to Jerusalem to present Him to the Lord in accordance with the Law of Moses. In the Temple, she meets the old Simeon, who takes the Christ Child in his arms and prophesies that He will be the light to the Gentiles, the glory of Israel, the rock of scandal for the perdition and salvation of many.

Let us ask the Most Holy Virgin for a fearless soul ablaze with love for Holy Mother Church, so that we also may be a light to our brethren and, if need be, a rock of scandal to our social circles.

Our Father: God's eternal wisdom.

10 Hail Marys:
1. Jesus and Mary's obedience to the Law.
2. Jesus' sacrifice of His humanity in the Temple.
3. Mary's sacrifice of her honor.
4. The joy and praise of Simeon and Anna the Prophetess.
5. The ransom of Jesus by the offering of two turtledoves.
6. The slaughter of the Holy Innocents by Herod in his cruelty.
7. The flight of Jesus into Egypt through Saint Joseph's obedience to the voice of the angel.
8. His mysterious stay in Egypt.
9. His return to Nazareth.
10. His growth in age and wisdom.

The FINDING *in the* TEMPLE

In this mystery we contemplate how the Virgin Mary, having lost her Son, found Him in the Temple after three days of wearisome search, listening to the Doctors of the Law and asking them questions.

Let us ask Mary Most Holy, by the merits of the anguish she suffered during her searching, to grant us an ever-increasing fidelity to the Church amidst the multiple perplexities that a faithful Catholic must undergo in our days.

Our Father: God's unfathomable sanctity.

10 Hail Marys:
1. Our Lord's hidden, laborious and obedient life in the house of Nazareth.
2. His preaching and finding in the Temple among the doctors.
3. His baptism by Saint John the Baptist.
4. His fasting and temptations in the desert.
5. His admirable preaching.
6. His astonishing miracles.
7. The selection of His twelve Apostles and the powers He gave them.
8. His marvellous transfiguration.
9. The washing of His Apostles' feet.
10. The institution of the Holy Eucharist.

FIRST SORROWFUL MYSTERY
The AGONY *in the* GARDEN

In this mystery we contemplate our Divine Redeemer praying in the Garden of Olives and sweating blood as He foresees the Passion He is to suffer. His apostles sleep.

Let us ask our dauntless Mother to remove from our souls all the cowardly optimism that invites us to sleep when we should be watching and praying, and to give us the virtue of seriousness so that we will courageously embrace suffering every time it comes our way.

Our Father: God's essential felicity.

10 Hail Marys:
1. The divine seclusions of Jesus Christ during His life, and especially His seclusion in the Garden of Olives.
2. His humble and fervent prayers during His life and on the eve of the Passion.
3. The patience and sweetness with which He bore His Apostles during His life and particularly in the Garden of Olives.
4. His soul's anxiety throughout His life and principally in the Garden of Olives.
5. The rivers of blood that sorrow caused to gush from His adorable being.
6. The consolation He willingly accepted from an angel during His agony.
7. His conformity to the will of His Father despite the aversion of His nature.
8. The valor with which He went to meet His executioners, and the force of the word with which He threw them to the ground and then raised them.
9. His betrayal by Judas and His arrest by the Jews.
10. His apostles' abandonment.

SECOND SORROWFUL MYSTERY
The SCOURGING *at the* PILLAR

In this mystery we contemplate Our Lord Jesus Christ bound to the pillar and mercilessly flogged at the order of Pilate, who wanted to please the crowd.

Let us ask the Mother of Divine Grace to give us, whenever we are beset by tribulation, the strength and perseverance shown by her Son as the blows of the lash tore into His undefiled flesh for our sins.

Our Father: God's admirable patience.

10 Hail Marys:
1. The chains and ropes that bound Jesus.
2. The blow He received in the house of Caiphas.
3. The denials of Saint Peter.
4. The ignominies He suffered in the house of Herod when the white robe was put on Him.
5. The removal of all His garments.
6. The scorn and insults He suffered from His executioners because of His nakedness.
7. The thorny rods and the cruel whips with which they beat and tore Him.
8. The pillar to which He was tied.
9. The blood He shed and the wounds He received.
10. His fall in His own blood out of weakness.

THIRD SORROWFUL MYSTERY
The CROWNING with THORNS

In this mystery we contemplate the King of kings despoiled of His garments and clothed in a scarlet cloak. He is crowned with thorns, crushed with blows, overwhelmed with affronts and outrages by the procurator's brutal soldiers.

Let us ask Mary Immaculate for an unshakable faith and at least a drop of the infinite dignity of Jesus when the wicked, with their laughter, mock our faithfulness to the morality of Holy Church.

Our Father: God's ineffable beauty.

10 Hail Marys:
1. The third stripping of Jesus.
2. His crown of thorns.
3. The cloth with which He was blindfolded.
4. The blows and spit with which His face was covered.
5. The old cloak placed on His shoulders.
6. The reed that was stuck in His hand.
7. The sharp stone on which He was seated.
8. The outrages and insults hurled at Him.
9. The blood and sweat that issued from His adorable head.
10. The hairs pulled from His head and beard.

FOURTH SORROWFUL MYSTERY
The CARRYING *of the* CROSS

In this mystery we contemplate our Divine Master – "the reproach of men and the Man of Sorrows" – bearing the crushing burden of the Cross, which tears His flesh and lays bare His bones.

By the shoulder wound of Christ, let us ask the Mother of Sorrows for the grace to proceed with supernatural determination in our spiritual lives and in our apostolate even when we fall under the weight of the cross.

Our Father: God's unlimited omnipotence.

10 Hail Marys:
1. Our Lord's presentation to the people with the "*Ecce Homo.*"
2. Barabbas being preferred to Our Lord.
3. The false witnesses brought against Him.
4. His condemnation to death.
5. The love with which He embraced and kissed His Cross.
6. The frightful pains He had while carrying it.
7. His falls from sheer weakness under its weight.
8. The painful meeting with His Holy Mother.
9. Veronica's veil, marked with the imprint of His face.
10. His tears and those of His Holy Mother and the pious women who accompanied Him to Calvary.

FIFTH SORROWFUL MYSTERY
The CRUCIFIXION

In this mystery we contemplate our Divine Savior nailed to the Cross and raised aloft between two thieves. He is plunged in an ocean of bitterness; He is abandoned by the Father Himself.

Let us ask the Blessed Mother, who stands at the foot of the Cross, to grant us the grace of taking our vocation to its last consequences and of loving the sacrifices it entails.

Our Father: God's frightful justice.

10 Hail Marys:
1. The five wounds of Jesus and the blood He shed on the Cross.
2. His pierced heart and the Cross upon which He was crucified.
3. The nails and lance that pierced Him, and the sponge of vinegar and gall given Him to drink.
4. The shame and infamy He suffered being crucified naked between two thieves.
5. The compassion of His Holy Mother.
6. His seven last words.
7. His abandonment and silence.
8. The affliction of the whole universe.
9. His cruel and ignominious death.
10. His taking down from the Cross and His burial.

FIRST GLORIOUS MYSTERY
The RESURRECTION

In this mystery we contemplate our Divine Redeemer rising through His own power on the third day. His body is in a state of glory: His wounds are now tokens of His triumph over death.

Let us ask Our Lady of Fatima for a staunch hope in the triumph of her Immaculate Heart and a jubilant enthusiasm in the anticipation of her kingdom.

Our Father: God's infinite eternity.

10 Hail Marys:
1. The descent of the soul of Our Lord into hell.
2. The joy of the souls of the holy fathers, and their departure from limbo.
3. The rejoining of His soul and body in the sepulcher.
4. His miraculous exit from the sepulcher.
5. His victories over death and sin, the world and the devil.
6. The four glorious qualities of His body.
7. The power in heaven and on earth that He received from His Father.
8. The apparitions with which He honored His Holy Mother, His Apostles and His disciples.
9. The conversations about heaven that He had with His Apostles, and the meal He partook with them.
10. The authority and mission He gave them to preach throughout the world.

SECOND GLORIOUS MYSTERY
The ASCENSION

In this mystery we contemplate the Just One withdrawing from His disciples and ascending into heaven forty days after His resurrection. it is the concluding work of redemption.

By this final elevation of Our Lord's human nature into the condition of divine glory, let us ask the Most Holy Virgin for the ultimate exaltation of Holy Mother Church and Christian civilization.

Our Father: God's boundless immensity.

10 Hail Marys:
1. The promise Jesus made to His Apostles that He would send them the Holy Ghost, and the order He gave them to prepare themselves to receive Him.
2. The gathering of all His disciples on Mount Olivet.
3. The blessing He gave them as He ascended from this earth to heaven.
4. His glorious and admirable ascension, by His own power, into the empyrean heaven.
5. The reception and divine triumph given Him by God, His Father, and the whole celestial court.
6. The triumphant power with which He opened the gates of heaven, where no mortal had ever entered.
7. His sitting at the right hand of His Father as His well-beloved Son and equal.
8. The power He received to judge the living and the dead.
9. His second coming, in which His might and majesty will appear in all their splendor.
10. The justice He will do in the Last Judgment, rewarding the good and chastising the evil for all eternity.

THIRD GLORIOUS MYSTERY
The DESCENT *of the* HOLY GHOST

In this mystery we contemplate Our Lord fulfilling His words to the Apostles: "I will ask the Father, and He shall give you another Paraclete, that He may abide with you forever" (John 14:16). The Apostles, gathered around Our Lady in the Cenacle, are now so filled with the Holy Ghost that they seem drunk (Acts 2:13).

Let us ask the Spouse of the Holy Ghost to say but a word and thus transform our weak, lukewarm and sinful souls.

Our Father: God's universal providence.

10 Hail Marys:
1. The truth of the Holy Ghost, God Who proceeds from the Father and the Son, and Who is the Heart of the Divinity.
2. The sending of the Holy Ghost by the Father and the Son to the Apostles.
3. The great noise with which He descended, a sign of His strength and power.
4. The tongues of fire He placed upon the Apostles to give them knowledge of the Scriptures, and love of God and neighbor.
5. The plenitude of graces with which He distinguished Mary, His faithful spouse.
6. His marvellous control over all the saints and over the person of Jesus Christ Himself, Whom He guided during His whole life.
7. The twelve fruits of the Holy Ghost.
8. The seven gifts of the Holy Ghost.
9. To request particularly the gift of wisdom and the coming of His reign over the hearts of men.
10. To obtain victory over the evil spirits opposed to Him; namely, the spirits of the world, the flesh and the devil.

FOURTH GLORIOUS MYSTERY
The ASSUMPTION

In this mystery we contemplate the Virgin Mary being taken body and soul into heaven by God amidst the rejoicing of the angels.

Let us ask our celestial Mother to fill us with faith and to make us pure and strong, so that we may fight worthily for her on earth and rejoice with her in heaven forever.

Our Father: God's indescribable generosity.

10 Hail Marys:
1. The eternal predestination of Mary as the masterpiece of God's hands.
2. Her Immaculate Conception, and her plenitude of grace and reason while within the womb of her mother, Saint Anne.
3. Her nativity, which gladdened the whole universe.
4. Her presentation and stay in the Temple.
5. Her admirable life exempt from all sin.
6. The fullness of her singular virtues.
7. Her fertile virginity and painless birth.
8. Her divine maternity and her alliance with the Most Holy Trinity.
9. Her precious and loving death.
10. Her resurrection and triumphant assumption.

FIFTH GLORIOUS MYSTERY
The CORONATION

In this mystery we contemplate the Daughter of God, the Mother of God, the Spouse of God, addressed in the words of the Canticle of Canticles "Come: thou shalt be crowned," and made empress and mistress of all creation.

Let us ask our Queen that, from the height of glory on which she was placed, she will be for us a Mother of Mercy, raising us when we fall, loving us at every moment, so that, like the angels, we may faithfully serve her in all things.

Our Father: God's inaccessible glory.

10 Hail Marys:
1. The triple crown with which the Most Holy Trinity crowned Mary.
2. The joy and new glory heaven received by her triumph.
3. To recognize her as Queen of Heaven and Earth, angels and men.
4. The treasurer of the graces of God, of the merits of Jesus Christ and of the gifts of the Holy Ghost.
5. The mediatrix and advocate of men.
6. The destroyer and ruin of the devil and of heresies.
7. The secure refuge of sinners.
8. The mother and nurturer of Christians.
9. The joy and sweetness of the just.
10. The universal refuge of the living, the all-powerful consolation of the afflicted, of the dying and of the souls in Purgatory.

The FIVE FIRST SATURDAYS *Devotion*

On December 10, 1925, Our Lady promised Sister Lucia she would "...assist at the hour of death, with the graces necessary for salvation, all those who on the first Saturdays of five consecutive months confess, receive Holy Communion, pray a rosary, and keep me company for a quarter of an hour meditating on the fifteen mysteries with the intention of offering me reparation."

Four requirements to faithfully fulfill the Five First Saturdays

1. Go to Confession.
2. Receive Holy Communion.
3. Say five decades of the Holy Rosary.
4. Meditate for a quarter of an hour on the fifteen mysteries of the rosary (separate from praying the rosary).

During an apparition on February 15, 1926, because of difficulty that some people had to be able to confess on a Saturday, Sister Lucia asked Our Lord if the confession would be valid if done within a period of eight days before or eight days after the first Saturday. Our Lord answered: "Yes, it can even be within many more days, provided they are in the state of grace when they receive Me, and have the intention of offering reparation to the Immaculate Heart of Mary."

Our Lord explained to Sister Lucia why five first Saturdays — there are five kinds of offenses and blasphemies committed against the Immaculate Heart of Mary:

1. Those committed against the Immaculate Conception
2. Those committed against the virginity of Our Lady
3. Those committed against the Divine maternity, refusing at the same time, to accept her as the mother of men
4. Those committed by men who publicly attempt to instill indifference, scorn, and even hatred for this Immaculate Mother in the hearts of children
5. Those committed by men who insult her directly in her sacred images.

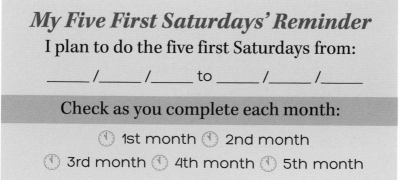

My Five First Saturdays' Reminder
I plan to do the five first Saturdays from:
_____ / _____ / _____ to _____ / _____ / _____

Check as you complete each month:
1st month 2nd month
3rd month 4th month 5th month

MORE *about the* ROSARY

In the following pages, you will find:

A BRIEF HISTORY *of the* ROSARY

The word "rosary" means crown of roses. In pre-Christian times, pagans used to crown their statues with roses to symbolize the rendering of their hearts to the gods. With the coming of Christianity, the fusing of their love for false gods with their hatred for the early Christians led to the Roman persecutions.

During these persecutions, Christian virgins, dressed in their best and crowned with roses, went to their martyrdom in the sandy arena of the Coliseum. Their brethren in the Faith later collected these crowns of roses and prayed before them, saying one prayer per rose.

Among these prayers, that which held the foremost place in Christian hearts from the beginning was the one that flowed from the lips of our Divine Redeemer Himself: the Our Father.

Little by little, as though to complement this most perfect prayer, the Holy Ghost inspired the faithful to address the Mother of the Redeemer with the words spoken by the angel and by Saint Elizabeth, giving rise to the recitation of the first part of the Hail Mary. The Church added the name of Mary to the beginning and that of Jesus to the end of this salutation.

At the Council of Ephesus, in 431, Holy Mother Church defined that the Blessed Virgin is truly the Mother of God and gave us the conclusion of the Hail Mary: "Holy Mary, Mother of God. . ." which officially became the second part of the Hail Mary in 1568.

Stained glass of Saint Dominic receiving the Rosary from Our Lady.

At the Council of Ephesus, in 431, Holy Mother Church defined that the Blessed Virgin is truly the Mother of God and gave us the conclusion of the Hail Mary: "Holy Mary, Mother of God..." which officially became the second part of the Hail Mary in 1568.

In the monasteries of the Middle Ages, the monks who could not read replaced the recitation of the Psalms with the repetition of the Our Father. Since there are 150 Psalms in the Bible, they prayed a series of 150 Our Fathers, which they called the "Psalter of Christ." To count the Our Fathers, the monks used knotted ropes or collars of grains, which in France came to be called "patenôtres."

In the eleventh century, some hermits and laymen began to recite "Our Lady's Psalter," that is, 150 salutations "Hail Mary... fruit of thy womb," instead of the 150 Our Fathers. They divided these salutations into three series of 50, which they termed "rosaries" or "crowns" because of the custom of crowning Our Lady's statues with flowers.

But it was only in 1214, according to a pious and admirable tradition, that the Most Holy Virgin herself consecrated this devotion by appearing to Saint Dominic of Guzman, founder of the Dominicans, and giving him the rosary in its present form as a weapon to combat the Albigensian heresy that was devastating southern France.

Let the great apostle of Mary, Saint Louis de Montfort, tell us the circumstances in which that great event took place:

"Saint Dominic, seeing that the gravity of people's sins was hindering the conversion of the Albigensians, withdrew into a forest near Toulouse where he prayed unceasingly for three days and three nights. During this time he did nothing but weep and do harsh penances in order to appease the anger of Almighty God. He used his discipline so much that his body was lacerated, and finally he fell into a coma.

"At this point Our Lady appeared to him, accompanied by three angels, and she said:

"'Dear Dominic, do you know which weapon the Blessed Trinity wants to use to reform the world?'

"'Oh, my Lady,' answered Saint Dominic, 'you know far better than I do because, next to your Son Jesus Christ, you have always been the chief instrument of our salvation.'

"Then Our Lady replied:

"'I want you to know that, in this kind of warfare, the battering ram has always been the Angelic Psalter which is the foundation stone of the New Testament. Therefore, if you want to reach these hardened souls and win them over to God, preach my Psalter.'

"So he arose, comforted, and burning with zeal for the conversion of the people in that district he made straight for the Cathedral. At once, unseen angels rang the bells to gather the people together and Saint Dominic began to preach.

"At the very beginning of his sermon an appalling storm broke out, the earth shook, the sun was darkened, and there was so much thunder and lightning that all were very much afraid. Even greater was their fear when, looking at a picture of Our Lady exposed in a prominent place, they saw her raise her arms to heaven three times to call down God's vengeance upon them if they failed to be converted, to amend their lives, and seek the protection of the Holy Mother of God.

"At last, at the prayer of Saint Dominic, the storm came to an end, and he went on preaching. So fervently and compellingly did he explain the importance and value of the Holy Rosary that almost all the people of Toulouse embraced it and renounced their false beliefs" (*The Secret of the Rosary*, Montfort Publications, Bay Shore, N.Y., 1954, pp. 18-19).

After this brilliant victory of the Faith, obtained by preaching the rosary, Saint Dominic endeavoured, with renewed fervor to spread such a meritorious devotion. But after his death, in 1221, as the memory of his preaching gradually faded in the minds of the Christians who had heard him, devotion to the rosary declined.

One century later it was practically buried and forgotten.

"I want you to know that, in this kind of warfare, the battering ram has always been the Angelic Psalter which is the foundation stone of the New Testament. Therefore, if you want to reach these hardened souls and win them over to God, preach my Psalter."

To re-establish this devotion in its pristine fervour, Our Lady chose Blessed Alan de la Roche, a Dominican from the monastery at Dinan, France. In 1464, after apparitions of Our Lord, Our Lady and Saint Dominic himself, Blessed Alan solemnly resolved to preach the rosary incessantly, which he did until his death in 1475, around the time of the founding of the Confraternity of the Holy Rosary at the Dominican convent at Cologne. It was to him and Saint Dominic that Our Lady gave her promises to those who pray the rosary. (These promises appear on page 71 of this book.)

The erection of confraternities in many other places led to the printing of numerous books on the rosary. The devotion quickly spread throughout Europe. It is to the confraternities that the acceptance of the list of fifteen mysteries to be meditated on during the recitation of the Hail Marys is mainly due. Pope Saint Pius V, a Dominican himself, enunciated the list in his *Consueverunt* of 1569.

By then, Europe was tragically menaced by the might of the Turkish Empire. Saint Pius V convoked a crusade to save Christendom. However, many Christian peoples, either rendered lukewarm by the Renaissance or alienated from the bosom of the Church by Protestantism, turned a deaf ear to the Pope. But the Holy Father did not rest until he had organized a fleet of about 200 galleys from the Papal States, Malta, Spain, Naples and Sicily, and the states of Venice and Genoa.

This Christian fleet, placed under the Most Holy Virgin's protection by the Pope, sailed under the command of Don Juan of Austria, half-brother of King Philip II of Spain. The Muslim fleet was sighted about 50 miles west of the harbor of Lepanto, which is just inside the narrow entrance of the Gulf of Corinth.

Battle was joined on October 7, 1571. Upon its outcome depended the future of Christendom.

Painting of the Battle of Lepanto in 1571.

During four long hours, galleys crashed into each other, musket balls and arrows flew everywhere, men swarmed aboard the enemy ships wherever they could get a grip.

Although things had gone badly for the Christians at first, in the end they were victorious. Ali Pasha, the commander in chief of the Muslim fleet, was killed and his standard taken. The Muslims, losing courage, began to flee.

The combat became a slaughter of infidels. It is reckoned that 24,000 Muslims were killed and 5,000 taken prisoner. The Christians captured 177 ships and freed perhaps as many as 15,000 Christian

rowers, slaves in the Turkish galleys.

On the day of the battle, Saint Pius V was working with the cardinals. Suddenly, interrupting his work and opening the window, he looked at the sky and cried out: "A truce to business; our great task at present is to thank God for the victory He has just given the Christian army."

More than two weeks later, a courier, delayed by storms at sea, arrived in Rome with the news of the naval victory of Lepanto. The Pope wept for joy: the power of Islam had been dealt a shattering blow from which it will hopefully never recover. To thank the Most Holy Virgin for this triumph obtained while the members of all the confraternities of Rome were holding rosary processions, Saint Pius V added to the Litany of the Blessed Virgin Mary the supplication "Help of Christians" and instituted for the first Sunday of October the feast of Our Lady of Victory, which was changed by Gregory XIII to the feast of the Most Holy Rosary.

After a new victory over the Turks gained by Prince Eugene of Savoy in 1716, at the Battle of Peterwardein in Hungary, Pope Clement XI extended the celebration of the feast of the rosary to the universal Church. The great Saint Pius X fixed the feast on October 7.

In 1917, less than three years after the death of Saint Pius X, Our Lady appeared to three shepherd children, Lucia, Francisco and Jacinta (aged ten, nine and seven respectively), at Cova da Iria, Fatima, Portugal, in a series of six apparitions that began May 13 and ended October 13. The authenticity of these apparitions was confirmed by the miracle of the sun witnessed by about 70,000 spectators during the final apparition.

At Fatima, Our Lady gave the three children the mission of telling the world that she was profoundly displeased with the impiety and corruption of men. She warned that if mankind did not amend its ways a terrible chastisement would come, several nations would be annihilated, Russia would spread its errors throughout the world and the Holy Father would have much to suffer.

In her message, the Queen of Heaven and Earth, along with pointing out the danger, tells us how to avoid it. She maternally provides guidelines to avert this terrible chastisement: she asks for prayer and penance, and especially the recitation of the Holy Rosary.

It was after giving the warning of the chastisement and the ways to avoid it that Our Lady taught us the prayer to be recited at the end of each mystery of the rosary. She told Lucia: "When you pray the rosary, after each decade say, 'O my Jesus, forgive us our sins, save us from the fire of hell; lead all souls to heaven, especially those in most need of Thy mercy.'"

At the tempestuous beginning of the twenty-first century, amidst the most devastating crisis in history, a beacon of hope shines in the words spoken by Our Lady at Fatima, for she has assured us: "Finally, my Immaculate Heart will triumph!"

Four STORIES of the HOLY ROSARY

The Lady from Rome

A certain pious but self-willed lady in Rome was so devout and fervent that she put to shame by her holy life even the strictest religious in the Church.

Having decided to ask Saint Dominic's advice about her spiritual life, she made her confession to him. For penance he gave her one rosary to say and advised her to say it every day. She excused herself, saying that she had her regular exercises, that she made the Stations of Rome every day, that she wore sack-cloth as well as a hair-shirt, that she gave herself the discipline several times a week, that she often fasted and did other penances. Saint Dominic urged her over and over again to take his advice and say the rosary, but she would not hear of it. She left the confessional, horrified at the methods of this new spiritual director who had tried so hard to persuade her to take up a devotion for which she had no taste.

Later on, when she was at prayer she fell into ecstasy and had a vision of her soul appearing before the Supreme Judge. Saint Michael put all her penances and other prayers on one side of the scales and all her sins and imperfections on the other. The tray of her good works were greatly outweighed by that of her sins and imperfections.

Filled with alarm, she cried for mercy, imploring the help of the Blessed Virgin, her gracious advocate, who took the one and only rosary she had said for her penance and dropped it on the tray of her good works. This one rosary was so heavy that it weighed more than all her sins as well as all her good works. Our Lady then reproved her for having refused to follow the counsel of her servant Dominic and for not saying the rosary every day.

As soon as she came to herself she rushed and threw herself at the feet of Saint Dominic and told him all that had happened, begged his forgiveness for her unbelief, and promised to say the rosary faithfully every day. By this means she rose to Christian perfection and finally to the glory of everlasting life.

TAKEN FROM THE SECRET OF THE ROSARY
BY SAINT LOUIS DE MONTFORT

The King and the Rosary

Alphonsus, King of Leon and Galicia, very much wanted all his servants to honor the Blessed Virgin by saying the rosary. So he used to hang a large rosary on his belt and always wore it, but unfortunately never said it himself. Nevertheless his wearing it encouraged his courtiers to say the rosary very devoutly.

One day the king fell seriously ill and when he was given up for dead he found himself, in a vision, before the judgment seat of Our Lord. Many devils were there accusing him of all the sins he had committed and Our Lord as Sovereign Judge was just about to condemn him to hell when Our Lady appeared to intercede for him.

She called for a pair of scales and had his sins placed in one of the balances, whereas she put the rosary that he had always worn on the other scale, together with all the rosaries that had been said because of his example. It was found that the rosaries weighed more than his sins.

Looking at him with great kindness Our Lady said: "As a reward for this little honor that you paid me in wearing my rosary, I have obtained a great grace for you from my Son.

Your life will be spared for a few more years. See that you spend these years wisely, and do penance."

When the king regained consciousness he cried out: "Blessed be the rosary of the Most Holy Virgin Mary, by which I have been delivered from eternal damnation!"

After he had recovered his health he spent the rest of his life in spreading devotion to the Holy Rosary and said it faithfully every day.

People who love the Blessed Virgin ought to follow the example of King Alphonsus and that of the saints whom I have mentioned so that they too may win other souls for the Confraternity of the Holy Rosary. They will then receive great graces on earth and eternal life later on. "They that explain me shall have life everlasting life." Ecclesiasticus (Sirach) 24:31 *Taken from the Secret of the Rosary by St. Louis de Montfort.*

Vienna Saved by the Rosary

Vienna, Austria—After World War II, Austria was divided between four countries: America, France, the United Kingdom, and Russia, which was still communist. The section of Austria controlled by the communists was the richest, and included the city of Vienna. The Viennese were subject to all the atrocities and tyrannies of communism.

With all of his country's problems weighing heavily on his heart, Capuchin Fr. Petrus Pavlicek made a pilgrimage to Mariazell, the principle Marian shrine in Austria. While deep in prayer before the miraculous image of Our Lady above the shrine's high altar, he was told by an interior voice: "Do as I say and there will be peace."

To obey this inspiration of Our Lady, Fr. Pavlicek founded the Holy Rosary Crusade of Reparation in 1947. His Crusade consisted of the Viennese faithful coming out of their homes in order to participate in a public rosary procession in the streets of the city. The intentions of the rosary were for the end of communism in their country and in the world. Father traveled throughout Austria with a statue of Our Lady of Fatima promoting the Rosary Crusade. At first, the processions were miniscule, but in time they grew to staggering proportions. The Prime Minister and other members of the Austrian government soon joined the ranks, along with all of the nation's bishops.

In 1955, after eight years spreading the word about the Crusade throughout Austria, the rosary processions would reach the size of half a million people, about one-tenth of the Austrian population.

Finally, through the help of Our Lady, the Soviet forces pulled out of Austria in October of 1955, leaving the country for good.

Each year on September 12th, the feast of the Holy Name of Mary, thousands gather in Vienna to thank the Mother of God for her intercession in freeing their country from communist domination.

The Rosary and the Coal Truck

It was a cold, wintry night in Ohio when homes used coal for fuel. One home had only enough to make it till dawn. Young Mary, who writes this story, tells us her family was going through hard times as her Dad had lost his job.

As she sat around the kitchen table with her parents, there was talk that she and her eight siblings might have to go to the Children's Home on the morrow. They could only hope the relief truck would come in the morning. But there was no guaranty. It was then they decided to say a rosary.

As they finished, there was the rumble of a motor in the

lane. The coal truck! Mary's Dad ran out to help unload. Back in, he remarked, "Funny, I've never seen that man, and he didn't give me a paper to sign or anything."

That night they slept warm, and worriless. But next morning there was the coal truck again. Mary's Mom informed the driver, a cousin, that they had a delivery the night before.

The cousin chuckled, "Mine is the only relief truck in the area. If you got a load last night, St Joseph must have brought it!"

Mary's family never knew who the delivery man was...

It didn't help that they never got a bill.

*Whoever shall have a true devotion
for the rosary shall not die without the
sacraments of the Church.*

The FIFTEEN PROMISES
of MARY MOST HOLY

to Those Who Pray the Rosary

1. Whoever shall faithfully serve me by the recitation of the rosary shall receive signal graces.
2. I promise my special protection and the greatest graces to all those who shall recite the rosary.
3. The rosary shall be a powerful armor against hell; it will destroy vice, decrease sin and defeat heresy.
4. It will cause virtue and good works to flourish; it will obtain for souls the abundant mercy of God; it will withdraw the hearts of men from the love of the world and its vanities, and will lift them to the desire of eternal things. Oh, that souls would sanctify themselves by this means!
5. The soul that recommends itself to me by the recitation of the rosary shall not perish.
6. Whoever shall recite the rosary devoutly, applying himself to the consideration of its sacred mysteries, shall never be conquered by misfortune: if he be a sinner, he shall not perish by an unprovided death; if he be just, he shall remain in the grace of God. He shall become worthy of eternal life.
7. Whoever shall have a true devotion for the rosary shall not die without the sacraments of the Church.
8. Those who are faithful to the recitation of the rosary shall have, during their life and at their death the light

of God and the plenitude of His graces. At the moment of death they shall participate in the merits of the saints in paradise.

9. I shall deliver from purgatory those who have been devoted to the rosary.

10. The faithful children of the rosary shall merit a high degree of glory in heaven.

11. You shall obtain all you ask of me by the recitation of the rosary.

12. All those who propagate the Holy Rosary shall be aided by me in their necessities.

13. I have obtained from my Divine Son that all the advocates of the rosary shall have for intercessors the entire celestial court during their life and at the hour of death.

14. All who recite the rosary are my sons, and brothers of My son, Jesus Christ.

15. Devotion to My rosary is a great sign of predestination.

Four ways *to* Avoid Distractions
During the Rosary

BY SAINT LOUIS DE MONTFORT

To be guilty of willful distractions during prayer would show a great lack of respect and reverence; it would make our rosaries unfruitful and make us guilty of sin.

How can we expect God to listen to us if we ourselves do not pay attention to what we are saying? How can we expect Him to be pleased if, while in the presence of His tremendous majesty, we give in to distractions, like a child running after a butterfly? People who do that forfeit God's blessing, which is changed into a curse for having treated the things of God disrespectfully: "Cursed be the one who does God's work negligently." Jer. 48:10.

Of course, you cannot say your rosary without having a few involuntary distractions; it is even difficult to say a Hail Mary without your imagination troubling you a little, for it is never still; but you can say it without voluntary distractions, and you must take all sorts of precautions to lessen involuntary distractions and to control your imagination.

Four Ways to Avoid Distractions
1. Put yourself in the presence of God and imagine that God and His Blessed Mother are watching you.
2. Imagine that your guardian angel is at your right hand,

taking your Hail Marys, if they are well said, and using them like roses to make crowns for Jesus and Mary.

3. Remember that at your left hand is the devil, ready to pounce on every Hail Mary that comes his way and to write it down in his book of death, if they are not said with attention, devotion, and reverence.

4. Do not fail to offer up each decade in honor of one of the mysteries, and try to form a picture in your mind of Jesus and Mary in connection with that mystery.

We read in the life of Blessed Hermann of the Order of the Premonstratensians, that at one time when he used to say the rosary attentively and devoutly while meditating on the mysteries, Our Lady used to appear to him resplendent in breathtaking majesty and beauty.

But, as time went on, his fervor cooled and he fell into the way of saying his rosary hurriedly and without giving it his full attention. Then one day Our Lady appeared to him again, but this time she was far from beautiful, and her face was furrowed and drawn with sadness.

Blessed Hermann was appalled at the change in her, and Our Lady explained, "This is how I look to you, Hermann, because this is how you are treating me; as a woman to be despised and of no importance. Why do you no longer greet me with respect and attention while meditating on my mysteries and praising my privileges?"

The Rosary Is the Hardest Prayer to Say Well

When the rosary is well said, it gives Jesus and Mary more glory and is more meritorious for the soul than any other prayer. But it is also the hardest prayer to say well and to persevere in, owing especially to the distractions which almost inevitably attend the constant repetition of the same words.

When we say the Little Office of Our Lady, or the Seven Penitential Psalms, or any prayers other than the rosary, the variety of words and expressions keeps us alert, prevents our imagination from wandering, and so makes it easier for us to say them well. On the contrary, because of the constant repetition of the Our Father and Hail Mary in the same unvarying form, it is difficult, while saying the rosary, not to become wearied and inclined to sleep, or to turn to other prayers that are more refreshing and less tedious.

This shows that one needs much greater devotion to persevere in saying the rosary than in saying any other prayer, even the Psalter of David.

Keeping the Imagination Focused

Our imagination, which is hardly still a minute, makes our task harder, and then of course there is the devil who never tires of trying to distract us and keep us from praying. To what ends does not the evil one go against us while we are engaged in saying our rosary against him.

Being human, we easily become tired and slipshod, but the devil makes these difficulties worse when we are saying the rosary. Before we even begin, he makes us feel bored, distracted, or exhausted; and when we have started praying, he oppresses us from all sides, and when after much difficulty and many distractions, we have finished, he whispers to us:

"What you have just said is worthless. It is useless for you to say the rosary. You had better get on with other things. It is only a waste of time to pray without paying attention to what you are saying; half-an-hour's meditation or some spiritual reading would be much better. Tomorrow, when you are not feeling so sluggish, you'll pray better; leave the rest of your rosary till then."

By tricks of this kind the devil gets us to give up the Rosary altogether or to say it less often, and we keep putting it off or change to some other devotion.

How to Defeat the Devil

Dear friend of the Rosary Confraternity, do not listen to the devil, but be of good heart, even if your imagination has been bothering you throughout your rosary, filling your mind with all kinds of distracting thoughts, so long as you tried your best to get rid of them as soon as you noticed them.

Always remember that the best rosary is the one with the most merit, and there is more merit in praying when it is hard than when it is easy. Prayer is all the harder when it is, naturally speaking, distasteful to the soul and is filled with those annoying little ants and flies running about in your imagination, against your will, and scarcely allowing you the time to enjoy a little peace and appreciate the beauty of what you are saying.

Even if you have to fight distractions all through your whole rosary, be sure to fight well, arms in hand: that is to say, do not stop saying your rosary even if it is difficult to say and you have no sensible devotion. It is a terrible battle, but one that is profitable to the faithful soul.

If you put down your arms, that is, if you give up the rosary, you will be admitting defeat and then the devil, having got what he wanted, will leave you in peace, and on the day of judgment will taunt you because of your faithlessness and lack of courage. "He who is faithful in little things will also be faithful in those that are greater." Luke 16:10.

He who is faithful in rejecting the smallest distractions

when he says even the smallest prayer, will also be faithful in great things. Nothing is more certain, since the Holy Spirit has told us so.

So all of you, servants and handmaids of Jesus Christ and the Blessed Virgin, who have made up your minds to say the rosary every day, be of good heart. Do not let the multitude of flies (as I call the distractions that make war on you during prayer) make you abandon the company of Jesus and Mary, in whose holy presence you are when saying the rosary. In what follows I shall give you suggestions for diminishing distractions in prayer.

More Helpful Ways to Avoid Distractions

After you have invoked the Holy Spirit, in order to say your rosary well, place yourself for a moment in the presence of God and make the offering of the decades in the way I will show you later.

Before beginning a decade, pause for a moment or two, depending on how much time you have, and contemplate the mystery that you are about to honor in that decade.

Always be sure to ask, by this mystery and through the intercession of the Blessed Virgin, for one of the virtues that shines forth most in this mystery or one of which you are in particular need.

Take great care to avoid the two pitfalls that most people fall into during the rosary. The first is the danger of not asking for any graces at all, so that if some good people were asked their rosary intention they would not know what to say. So, whenever you say your rosary, be sure to ask for some special grace or virtue, or strength to overcome some sin.

The second fault commonly committed in saying the rosary is to have no intention other than that of getting it over with as quickly as possible. This is because so many look upon the rosary as a burden, which weighs heavily upon them when it has not been said, especially when we have promised to say it regularly or have been told to say it as a penance more or less against our will.